D0845903

Pebble® Plus

Dogs, Dogs, Dogs

All about Poodles

by Erika L. Shores

Consulting Editor: Gail Saunders-Smith, PhD

CAPSTONE PRESS
a capstone imprint

Pebble Plus is published by Capstone Press,
1710 Roe Crest Drive, North Mankato, Minnesota 56003.
www.capstonepub.com

Library of Congress Cataloging-in-Publication Data
Shores, Erika L., 1976–
All about poodles / by Erika L. Shores.
p. cm.—(Pebble plus. Dogs, dogs, dogs)
Includes bibliographical references and index.
Summary: "Full-color photographs and simple text provide a brief introduction to poodles"—Provided by publisher.
ISBN 978-1-4296-8727-0 (library binding)
ISBN 978-1-62065-295-4 (ebook PDF)
1. Poodles—Juvenile literature. I. Title.
SF429.P85S54 2013
636.72'8—dc23

2011049822

Editorial Credits
Juliette Peters, designer; Marcie Spence, media researcher; Kathy McColley, production specialist

Photo Credits
123RF: Ray Woo, 21, Sally Wallis: 11; Alamy: imagebroker, cover; Capstone Studio: Karon Dubke, 9, 17; Corbis: Dale
C. Spartas, 7; Dreamstime: Pixbilder, 3, 15; Fiona Green: 1; iStockphoto: JanaLynn, 19, majorosl, 5; Shutterstock:
Natalia V Guseva, 13,

Note to Parents and Teachers

The Dogs, Dogs, Dogs series supports national science standards related to life science. This
book describes and illustrates poodles. The images support early readers in understanding
the text. The repetition of words and phrases helps early readers learn new words. This book
also introduces early readers to subject-specific vocabulary words, which are defined in the
Glossary section. Early readers may need assistance to read some words and to use the Table of
Contents, Glossary, Read More, Internet Sites, and Index sections of the book.

Printed in the United States of America in North Mankato, Minnestoa.
042013   007304R

Table of Contents

Fancy Dogs

Poodles look fancy with

their poofy hair and pretty bows.

Many poodle owners enter

their pets in dog shows.

Poodles are more than show dogs.

People first bred poodles to be

duck-hunting dogs. The dogs

easily swim through cold water

to bring back dead birds.

The Poodle Look

Poodles come in three sizes.

Standard poodles are the biggest.

Toy poodles are the smallest.

Miniature poodles are in between.

All poodles are as tall as they are long. Standard poodles can be 27 inches (69 centimeters) tall. Toy poodles are less than 10 inches (25 centimeters) tall.

Most poodles have white, black, or brown coats. Poodles competing in dog shows are shaved in spots. Balls of puffy hair are left on their ankles, hips, and tails.

Puppy Time

Three to five poodle puppies

are born in a litter.

Puppies have soft, wavy coats.

Their hair curls tighter

as they grow older.

Doggie Duties

With good care a poodle can live 15 years or longer. Owners feed, walk, and play with their poodles every day.

A poodle's thick, curly coat is always growing. Poodles need haircuts and regular brushing. If it isn't brushed, poodle hair can tangle and become matted.

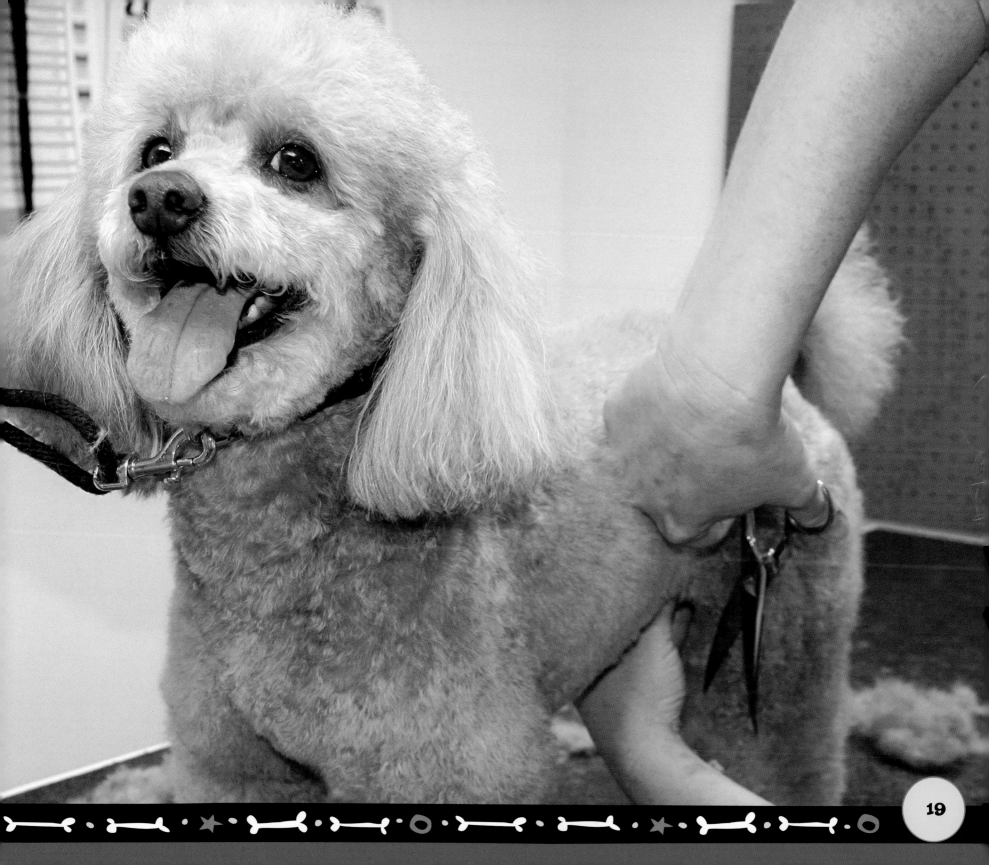

Perfect Pets

Smart, playful poodles make great pets. Poodles also don't shed as much as other breeds. People with pet allergies often aren't bothered by poodles.

Glossary

allergy—a reaction such as a runny nose, watery eyes, or a rash when around, or when eating, certain things; people may have allergies to animals, plants, dust, or certain kinds of food

breed—a certain kind of animal within an animal group; breed also means to raise a certain kind of animal

coat—an animal's hair or fur

dog show—a competition where judges pick the best dog in several events

litter—a group of animals born at the same time to the same mother

mat—to stick together in a clump

shed—to drop or fall off

tangle—to twist together

Read More

Hutmacher, Kimberly M. *I Want a Dog.* I Want a Pet. Mankato, Minn.: Capstone Press, 2012.

Mathea, Heidi. *Poodles.* Dogs. Edina, Minn.: ABDO Pub. Co., 2011.

Schuh, Mari. *Poodles.* Dog Breeds. Minneapolis: Bellwether Media, 2009.

Internet Sites

FactHound offers a safe, fun way to find Internet sites related to this book. All of the sites on FactHound have been researched by our staff.

Here's all you do:

Visit *www.facthound.com*

Type in this code: 9781429687270

Super-cool stuff! Check out projects, games and lots more at **www.capstonekids.com**

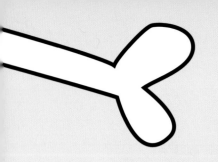

Index

Word Count: 215
Grade: 1
Early-Intervention Level: 16